Published by Creative Education
P.O. Box 227, Mankato, Minnesota 56002
Creative Education is an imprint of The Creative Company

Design by Stephanie Blumenthal; Production by The Design Lab
Printed in the United States of America

Photographs by Tom Stack & Associates (Erwin & Peggy Bauer, W. Perry Conway, Jeff Foott,
Thomas Kitchin, Joe McDonald, Mark Newman, John Shaw, Spencer Swanger)
Copyright © 2008 Creative Education
International copyright reserved in all countries. No part of this book may be reproduced in any form
without written permission from the publisher.

Library of Congress Cataloging-in-Publication Data
Frisch, Aaron.
Tundra / by Aaron Frisch.
p. cm. — (Our world)
Includes index.
ISBN 978-1-58341-574-0
1. Tundra ecology—Juvenile literature. 2. Tundras—Juvenile literature. I. Title
QH541.5.T8F75 2008   577.5'86—dc22   2006102992

First edition
2 4 6 8 9 7 5 3 1

OUR WORLD

T
U
N
D
R
A

Aaron Frisch

The tundra is a land close to the North Pole. There are not many trees on the tundra. Most of the land is flat. There are mountains in some places.

The tundra has two main **seasons**. They are winter and summer. In September, it becomes winter on the tundra. It is very cold then. But it does not snow very much.

The tundra often looks white and brown

The sun does not shine much on the tundra in the winter. In the middle of the winter, the sun does not come up at all! It is always nighttime. Sometimes there are **northern lights** in the sky. They make the sky colorful.

The northern lights can be many colors

In March, it becomes summer on the tundra. The sun shines longer. It gets warmer. In the middle of the summer, the sun never goes down! It is daytime for many days in a row.

Animals and plants come out in the summer

Even in the summer, it is not hot on the tundra. The ground is always partly frozen. When snow melts, the water cannot go into the ground. It makes big puddles.

Tundra snow melts in the summer

Plants and lichens make the ground pretty

Only little plants grow on the tundra. Grass and **moss** grow there. So do many flowers. There are lots of lichens *(LY-kens)* on the tundra. Lichens are not plants. They are things that grow on the ground. They look bumpy or like old paint.

Lots of animals live on the tundra. **Musk oxen** and polar bears live there. Furry animals called lemmings live there, too. So do birds called ptarmigans (*TAR-mih-gens*).

Tundra animals have thick fur or feathers

More animals live on the tundra in the summer. **Caribou** live there in the summer. They eat lichens and grass. Ducks and other birds fly to the tundra in the summer. There are bugs like butterflies, too.

Caribou eat a lot in the summer

The tundra is bright and busy in the summer. But when it becomes winter, many animals leave. The animals that stay wait a long time for summer to come again!

Many tundra animals are white

Go outside in the middle of the day, when the sun is high in the sky. How warm does it feel? Go outside again later, when the sun is low. How warm does it feel now? The sun feels the warmest when it is high. The sun is always low on the tundra. That is why it never gets hot there.

GLOSSARY

caribou—big deer that have long antlers

moss—flat plants that look like carpet

musk oxen—big animals that eat plants and have thick fur

northern lights—colorful lights that sometimes show in the sky at night

seasons—different times of the year; some seasons are colder and darker than other seasons

LEARN MORE ABOUT THE TUNDRA

Enchanted Learning
http://www.enchantedlearning.com/biomes/tundra/tundra.shtml
This site has lots of pictures of tundra animals.

Missouri Botanical Garden
http://www.mbgnet.net/sets/tundra/index.htm
This site has all kinds of facts about the tundra.

INDEX

animals 16, 18, 20
birds 16, 18
frozen ground 13
insects 18
lichens 15, 18
mountains 5
northern lights 8
plants 5, 15, 18
summer 6, 10, 13, 18, 20
sunshine 8, 10, 22
water 13
winter 6, 20